NEW BATS
IN OLD BELFRIES

TO

THE WARDEN

IN MEMORY

OF

NICHOLAS AND DOROTHY

WADHAM

NEW BATS
IN · OLD BELFRIES

POEMS

BY
JOHN BETJEMAN

```
1  2  2  4  4  5  5  3  3  1  1
2  1  4  2  5  4  3  5  1  3  2
3  4  1  5  2  3  4  1.5  2  3
4  3  5  1  3  2  1  4  2  5  4
5  5  3  3  1  1  2  2  4  4  5
```

LONDON
JOHN MURRAY, ALBEMARLE STREET, W.
1945

Poems by the same Author .

CONTINUAL DEW

OLD LIGHTS FOR NEW CHANCELS

ACKNOWLEDGMENTS

THE author wishes to thank the Editors of *Horizon,* the *Cornhill,* the *English Review,* the *Listener* and the *New Statesman and Nation* for permission to reprint some of the poems in this book. He is indebted to Colonel Kolkhorst for much help and encouragement and to N. Coghill, Esq., for assistance in selection.

Made and Printed in Great Britain by
Butler & Tanner Ltd., Frome and London

Contents

v

CONTENTS

Henley-on-Thames

I SEE the winding water make
A short and then a shorter lake
    As here stand I,
    And house-boat high,
Survey the Upper Thames.
  By sun the mud is amber-dyed
  In ripples slow and flat and wide,
   That flap against the house-boat side
And flop away in gems.

In mud and elder-scented shade
A reach away the breach is made
    By dive and shout
    That circles out
To Henley Tower and Town ;
  And " boats for hire " the rafters ring,
  And pink on white the roses cling,
  And red the bright geraniums swing
In baskets dangling down.

HENLEY-ON-THAMES

Oh shall I see the Thames again ?

The prow-promoted gems again,

    As beefy ATS

    Without their hats

Come shooting through the bridge ?

  And " cheerioh " or " cheeri-bye "

  Across the waste of waters die,

  And low the mists of evening lie

And lightly skims the midge.

Parliament Hill Fields

RUMBLING under blackened girders, Midland,
    bound for Cricklewood,
Puffed its sulphur to the sunset where that
    Land of Laundries stood.
Rumble under, thunder over, train and tram
    alternate go,
Shake the floor and smudge the ledger, Char-
    rington, Sells, Dale and Co.,
Nuts and nuggets in the window, trucks along
    the lines below.

When the Bon Marché was shuttered, when the
    feet were hot and tired,
Outside Charrington's we waited, by the
    "STOP HERE IF REQUIRED,"
Launched aboard the shopping basket, sat
    precipitately down,
Rocked past Zwanziger the Baker's, and the
    terrace blackish brown,
And the Anglo, Anglo-Norman Parish Church
    of Kentish Town.

Till the tram went over thirty, sighting terminus
    again,
Past municipal lawn tennis and the bobble-
    hanging plane ;
Soft the light suburban evening caught our
    ashlar-speckled spire,
Eighteen-sixty · Early English, as the mighty
    elms retire
Either side of Brookfield Mansions flashing fine
    French-window fire.

Oh the after tram ride quiet, when we heard,
    a mile beyond,
Silver music from the bandstand, barking dogs
    by Highgate Pond ;
Up the hill where stucco houses in Virginia
    creeper drown ;
And my childish wave of pity, seeing children
    carrying down
Sheaves of drooping dandelions to the courts of
    Kentish Town.

A Subaltern's Love-song

Miss J. HUNTER DUNN, Miss J. Hunter Dunn,
Furnish'd and burnish'd by Aldershot sun,
What strenuous singles we played after tea,
We in the tournament—you against me.

Love-thirty, love-forty, oh ! weakness of joy,
The speed of a swallow, the grace of a boy,
With carefullest carelessness, gaily you won,
I am weak from your loveliness, Joan Hunter
  Dunn.

Miss Joan Hunter Dunn, Miss Joan Hunter
  Dunn,
How mad I am, sad I am, glad that you won.
The warm-handled racket is back in its press,
But my shock-headed victor, she loves me no less.

Her father's euonymus shines as we walk,
And swing past the summerhouse, buried in talk,
And cool the verandah that welcomes us in
To the six-o'clock news and a lime juice and gin.

A SUBALTERN'S LOVE-SONG

The scent of the conifers, sound of the bath,
The view from my bedroom of moss-dappled
    path,
As I struggle with double-end evening tie,
For we dance at the Golf Club, my victor and I.

On the floor of her bedroom lie blazer and shorts
And the cream-coloured walls are be-trophied
    with sports,
And westering, questioning settles the sun
On your low-leaded window, Miss Joan Hunter
    Dunn.

The Hillman is waiting, the light's in the hall,
The pictures of Egypt are bright on the wall,
My sweet, I am standing beside the oak stair
And there on the landing's the light on your
    hair.

By roads " not adopted," by woodlanded ways
She drove to the club in the late summer haze,
Into nine-o'clock Camberley, heavy with bells
And mushroomy, pinewoody evergreen smells.

A SUBALTERN'S LOVE-SONG

Miss Joan Hunter Dunn, Miss Joan Hunter
    Dunn,
I can hear from the car park the dance has
    begun.
Oh ! full Surrey twilight ! importunate band !
Oh ! strongly adorable tennis girl's hand.

Around us are Rovers and Austins afar,
Above us, the intimate roof of the car,
And here on my right is the girl of my choice,
With the tilt of her nose and the chime of her
    voice,

And the scent of her wrap, and the words never
    said,
And the ominous, ominous dancing ahead.
We sat in the car park till quarter to one
And now I'm engaged to Miss Joan Hunter
    Dunn.

South London Sketch, 1844

LAVENDER SWEEP is drowned in Wandsworth,
　　Drowned in jessamine up to the neck,
Beetles sway upon bending grass leagues
　　Shoulder-level to Tooting Bec.
Rich as Middlesex, rich in signboards,
　　Lie the lover-trod lanes between,
Red Man, Green Man, Horse and Waggoner,
　　Elms and sycamores round a green.
Burst, good June, with a rush this morning,
　　Bindweed weave me an emerald rope
Sun, shine bright on the blossoming trellises,
　　June and lavender, bring me hope.

South London Sketch, 1944

FROM Bermondsey to Wandsworth
    So many churches are,
Some with apsidal chancels,
    Some Perpendicular
And schools by E. R. Robson
    In the style of Norman Shaw
Where blue-serged adolescence learn'd
    To model and to draw.

Oh, in among the houses,
    The viaduct below,
Stood the Coffee Essence Factory
    Of Robinson and Co.
Burnt and brown and tumbled down
    And done with years ago
Where the waters of the Wandle do
    Lugubriously flow.

SOUTH LONDON SKETCH, 1944

From dust of dead explosions,
   From scarlet-hearted fires,
All unconcerned this train draws in
   And smoothly that retires
And calmly rise on smoky skies
   Of intersected wires
The Nonconformist spirelets
   And the Church of England spires.

Bristol

GREEN upon the flooded Avon shone the after-
 storm-wet sky
Quick the struggling withy branches let the
 leaves of Autumn fly
And a star shone over Bristol, wonderfully far
 and high.

Ringers in an oil-lit belfry,—Bitton ? Kelston ?
 who shall say ?
Smoothly practising a plain course, caverned
 out the dying day
As their melancholy music flooded up and
 ebbed away.

Then all Somerset was round me and I saw the
 clippers ride,
High above the moonlit houses, triplemasted
 on the tide,
By the tall embattled church towers of the
 Bristol waterside.

And an undersong to branches dripping into
    pools and wells
Out of multitudes of elm trees over leagues of
    hills and dells
Was the mathematic pattern of a plain course
    on the bells.*

```
*1  2  2  4  4  5  5  3  3  1  1
 2  1  4  2  5  4  3  5  1  3  2
 3  4  1  5  2  3  4  1  5  2  3
 4  3  5  1  3  2  1  4  2  5  4
 5  5  3  3  1  1  2  2  4  4  5
```

On an Old-fashioned Water-colour of Oxford (early twentieth-century date)

SHINES, billowing cold and gold from Cumnor
    Hurst,
  A winter sunset on wet cobbles, where
  By Canterbury Gate the fishtails flare.
Someone in Corpus reading for a first
Pulls down red blinds and flounders on,
    immers'd
  In Hegel, heedless of the yellow glare
  On porch and pinnacle and window square,
The brown stone crumbling where the showers
    have burst.

A late, last luncheon staggers out of Peck
  And hires a hansom : from half-flooded grass
    Returning athletes bark at what they see.
But we will mount the horse-tram's upper deck
  And wave salute to Buols', as we pass
    Bound for the Banbury Road in time for tea.

A Lincolnshire Tale

KIRKBY with Muckby-cum-Sparrowby-cum-
    Spinx
Is down a long lane in the county of Lincs,
And often on Wednesdays, well-harnessed and
    spruce
I would drive into Wiss over Winderby Sluice.

A whacking great sunset bathed level and drain
From Kirkby with Muckby to Beckby-on-Bain,
And I saw, as I journeyed, my marketing done,
Old Caistorby tower take the last of the sun.

The night air grew nippy. An Autumn mist
    roll'd
(In a scent of dead cabbages) down from the
    wold
In the ocean of silence that flooded me round
The crunch of the wheels was a comforting
    sound.

A LINCOLNSHIRE TALE

The lane winded narrowly into the night
With the Bain on its left bank, the drain on its
   right,
And feebly the carriage lamps glimmered ahead
When all of a sudden *the pony fell dead.*

The remoteness was awful, the stillness intense.
Of invisible fenland, around and immense
And out on the dark, with a roar and a swell,
Swung, hollowly thundering, Speckleby bell.

Though myself the Archdeacon for many a
   year,
I had not summoned courage for visiting here
Since of all our incumbents, eccentric or sad,
The Speckleby Rector was said to be Mad.

Oh cold was the ev'ning and near was the tower
And strangely compelling the tenor bell's power !
As loud on the reed beds and strong through
   the dark
It toll'd from the church in the tenantless park.

The mansion was ruined, the empty demesne
Was slowly reverting to marshland again,
Marsh where the village was, grass in the Hall,
But the church and the Rectory left of it all.

And even in Springtime with kingcups about
And the stumps of some oak-trees attempting
    to sprout,
'Twas a sinister place, neither fenland nor
    wold,
And doubly forbidding in darkness and cold.

As down swung the tenor, a beacon of sound,
Over listening acres of waterlogged ground
I stood by the tombs to see pass and repass
The gleam of a taper, through clear leaded-
    glass.

Such a lighting of lights in the thunderous roar
That heart summoned courage to hand at the
    door
And grated it open on scents I knew well,
The dry smell of damp rot, the hassocky smell.

A LINCOLNSHIRE TALE

What a forest of woodwork in ochres and
    grains
Unevenly doubled in diamonded panes,
And over the plaster, so textured with time,
Sweet discoloration of umber and lime.

The candles ensconced on each high panelled-
    pew
Brought the caverns of baize that they lighted
    to view,
But the roof and its rafters were lost to the
    sight
As though sharing the dark of the Lincolnshire
    night :

And high from the chancel arch, paused to look
    down
A signpainter's beasts in their fight for the
    Crown
While massive, impressive and still as the grave
A three-decker pulpit frowned over the
    nave.

Shall I ever forget what a stillness was there
When the bell ceased its tolling and thinned on
  the air,
And an opening door shewed a long pair of hands
And the Rector himself in his gown and his
  bands.

Such a fell Visitation I shall not forget
Such a rush through the dark, that I rush
  through it yet,
Oh, I pray as the bells ring o'er fenland and hill
That the Speckleby acres are tenantless still.

St. Barnabas, Oxford

How long was the peril, how breathless the
. day,
In topaz and beryl, the sun dies away,
His rays lying static at quarter to six
On polychromatical lacing of bricks.
Good Lord, as the angelus floats down the
road,
Byzantine St. Barnabas, be Thine Abode.

Where once the fritillaries hung in the grass
A baldachin pillar is guarding the Mass.
Farewell to blue meadows we loved not
enough,
And elms in whose shadows were Glanville
and Clough
Not poets but clergymen hastened to meet
Thy redden'd remorselessness, Cardigan Street.

The Archæological Picnic

In this high pasturage, the Blunden time,
With Lady's Finger, Smokewort, Lovers' Loss,
And lin-lan-lone a Tennysonian chime
Stirring the sorrel and the gold-starred moss,
Cool is the chancel, bright the Altar cross.

Drink, Mary, drink your fizzy lemonade
And leave the king-cups. Take your grey felt
    hat ;
Here, where the low-side window lends a shade,
There, where the key lies underneath the mat
The rude forefathers of the hamlet sat.

Sweet smell of cerements and cold wet stones,
Hassock and cassock, paraffin and pew,
Green in a light which that sublime Burne Jones
White-hot and wondering from the glass kiln
    drew
Gleams and re-gleams this Trans arcade anew.

THE ARCHÆOLOGICAL PICNIC

So stand you waiting, freckled innocence !
For me the squinch and squint and Trans arcade ;
For you, where meadow grass is evidence,
With flattened pattern, of our picnic made,
One bottle more of fizzy lemonade.

May-day Song for North Oxford
(*Annie Laurie Tune*)

BELBROUGHTON ROAD is bonny, and pinkly
    bursts the spray
Of prunus and forsythia across the public way,
For a full spring-tide of blossom seethed and
    departed hence,
Leaving land-locked pools of jonquils by sunny
    garden fence.

And a constant sound of flushing runneth from
    windows where
The toothbrush too is airing in this new North
    Oxford air
From Summerfields to Lynam's, the thirsty
    tarmac dries,
And a Cherwell mist dissolveth on elm-
    discovering skies.

Oh! well-bound Wells and Bridges! Oh!
    earnest ethical search
For the wide high-table $\lambda o \gamma o \varsigma$ of St. C. S.
    Lewis's Church.

MAY-DAY SONG FOR NORTH OXFORD

This diamond-eyed Spring morning my soul
    soars up the slope
Of a right good rough-cast buttress on the
    housewall of my hope.

And open-necked and freckled, where once
    there grazed the cows,
Emancipated children swing on old apple
    boughs,
And pastel-shaded book rooms bring New Ideas
    to birth
As the whitening hawthorn only hears the
    heart beat of the earth.

Anticipation in Spring

STILL heavy with May, and the sky ready to
fall,

Meadows buttercup high, shed and chicken and
wire ?

And here where the wind leans on a sycamore silver wall,

Are you still taller than sycamores, gallant
Victorian spire ?

Still, fairly intact, and demolishing squads
about,

Bracketed station lamp with your oil-light
taken away ?

Weep flowering current, while your bitter cas-
cades are out,

Born in an age of railways, for flowering into
to-day !

Ireland with Emily

BELLS are booming down the bohreens,
  White the mist along the grass.
Now the Julias, Maeves and Maureens
  Move between the fields to Mass.
Twisted trees of small green apple
Guard the decent whitewashed chapel,
Gilded gates and grained oak doorway
Through them both, the rich and poor way,
  Small—and smaller—holders pass.

Say how many congregations
  On the broidered vestment gaze ?
Murmur past the painted stations
  As Thy Sacred Heart displays
Lush Kildare of scented meadows,
Roscommon, thin in ash tree shadows,
And Westmeath the lake reflected,
Spreading Leix the hill protected,
  Kneeling all in silver haze ?

25

In yews and woodbine, walls and guelder,
   Nettle-deep the faithful rest,
Winding leagues of flowering elder,
   Sycamore with ivy dressed,
Ruins in demesnes deserted,
Bog-surrounded bramble-skirted—
Townlands rich or townlands mean as
These, oh, counties of them screen us
   In the Kingdom of the West.

Stony seaboard, far and foreign,
   Stony hills poured over space,
Stony outcrop of the Burren,
   Stones in every fertile place,
Little fields with boulders dotted,
Grey-stone shoulders saffron-spotted,
Stone-walled cabins thatched with reeds,
Where a Stone Age people breeds
   The last of Europe's stone age race.

Has it held, the warm June weather?
   Draining shallow seapools dry,
When we bicycled together
   Down the bohreens fuchsia-high.

Till there rose, abrupt and lonely,

A ruined abbey, chancel only,

Lichen-crusted, time-befriended,

Soared the arches, splayed and splendid,

  · Romanesque against the sky.

In walled and pinnacled protection,

  One extinguished family waits

A Church of Ireland resurrection

  By the broken, rusty gates.

Sheepswool, straw and droppings cover,

Graves of spinster, rake and lover,

Whose fantastic mausoleum

Sings its own seablown Te Deum,

  In and out the slipping slates.

Margate

FROM out the Queen's Highcliffe for weeks at
  a stretch
I watched how the mower evaded the vetch,
So that over the putting course rashes were
  seen
Of pink and of yellow among the burnt green.

How restful to putt, when the strains of a
  band
Announced a *thé dansant* was on at the Grand,
While over the privet, comminglingly clear,
I heard lesser " Co-Optimists " down by the
  pier.

Then east-facing terraces rested in shade
And fluttered with bathing things gaily dis-
  played,
As though loth to admit that a sun or a planet
Could ever forsake any corner of Thanet.

MARGATE

How lightly municipal, meltingly tarr'd
Were the walks through the Lawns by the
    Queen's Promenade
As soft over Cliftonville languished the light
Down Harold Road, Norfolk Road into the
    night.

Oh ! then what a pleasure to see the ground
    floor
With tables for two laid as tables for four,
And bottles of sauce and Kia-Ora * and squash
Awaiting their owners who'd gone up to
    wash,—

Who had gone up to wash the ozone from their
    skins
The sand from their legs and the Rock from
    their chins
To prepare for an evening of dancing and
    cards
And forget the sea-breeze on the dry
    promenades.

* Pronounced " Kee-ora."

29

MARGATE

From third floor and fourth floor the children
    looked down
Upon ribbons of light in the salt-scented town ;
And more loud than the trams was the roar of
    the sea
As it washed in the shingle the scraps of
    their tea.

Beside the Queen's Highcliffe now rank grows
    the vetch,
Now dark is the terrace, a storm-battered
    stretch ;
And I think, as the fairy-lit sights I recall,
It is these we are fighting for, foremost of all.

Invasion Exercise on the Poultry Farm

SOFTLY croons the radiogram, loudly hoot
the owls
Judy gives the door a slam and goes to feed
the fowls.
Marty rolls a Craven A around her ruby lips
And runs her yellow fingers down her cor-
duroyded hips,
Shuts her mouth and screws her eyes and puffs
her fag alight
And hears some most peculiar cries that echo
through the night.

Ting-a-ling the telephone, to-whit to-whoo the
owls,
Judy, Judy, Judy girl, and have you fed the
fowls ?
No answer as the poultry gate is swinging there
ajar.
Boom the bombers overhead, between the
clouds a star,

And just outside, among the arks, in a shadowy
    sheltered place

Lie Judy and a paratroop in horrible em-
    brace.

Ting-a-ling the telephone, "Yes, this is Marty
    Hayne."

"Have you seen a paratroop come walking
    down your lane ?

He may be on your premises, he may be some-
    where near,

And if he is report the fact to Major Maxton-
    Weir."

White with rage and lined with age but strong
    and sturdy still

Marty now co-ordinates her passions and her
    will,

She will teach that Judy girl to trifle with the
    heart

And go and kiss a paratroop like any common
    tart.

She switches up the radiogram and covered by
    the blare

Marty gets a riding whip and whirls it in the air,

INVASION EXERCISE ON THE POULTRY FARM

She fetches down a length of rope and rushes,
    breathing hard
To let the couple have it for embracing in the
    yard.
Crack! the pair are paralysed. Click! they
    cannot stir.
Zip! she's trussed the paratroop. There's no
    embracing *her*.
Hullo, hullo, hullo, hullo . . . Major Maxton-
    Weir?
I trussed your missing paratroop. He's wait-
    ing for you here.

The Planster's Vision

Cut down that timber ! Bells, too many and
    strong,
      Pouring their music through the branches
      bare,
      From moon-white church-towers down the
      windy air
Have pealed the centuries out with Evensong.
Remove those cottages, a huddled throng !
      Too many babies have been born in there,
      Too many coffins, bumping down the stair,
Carried the old their garden paths along.

I have a Vision of The Future, chum,
      The workers' flats in fields of soya beans
        Tower up like silver pencils, score on score :
And Surging Millions hear the Challenge come
      From microphones in communal canteens
        "No Right ! No Wrong ! All's perfect,
        evermore."

In a Bath Teashop

"LET us not speak, for the love we bear one
    another—
    Let us hold hands and look."
She, such a very ordinary little woman;
    He, such a thumping crook;
But both, for the moment, little lower than the
    angels
    In the teashop's inglenook.

Before the Anæsthetic,

or

A Real Fright

INTOLERABLY sad, profound
St. Giles's bells are ringing round,
They bring the slanting summer rain
To tap the chestnut boughs again
Whose shadowy cave of rainy leaves
The gusty belfry-song receives.
Intolerably sad and true,
Victorian red and jewel blue,
The mellow bells are ringing round
And charge the evening light with sound,
And I look motionless from bed
On heavy trees and purple red
And hear the midland bricks and tiles
Throw back the bells of stone St. Giles,
Bells, ancient now as castle walls,
Now hard and new as pitchpine stalls
Now full with help from ages past
Now dull with death and hell at last.

Swing up ! and give me hope of life,

Swing down ! and plunge the surgeon's knife.

I, breathing for a moment, see

Death wing himself away from me

And think, as on this bed I lie

Is it extinction when I die ?

I move my limbs and use my sight ;

Not yet, thank God, not yet the Night.

Oh better far those echoing hells

Half-promised in the pealing bells

Than that this "I" should cease to be

Come quickly Lord, come quick to me.

St. Giles's bells are asking now

"And has thou known the Lord, hast thou ? "

St. Giles's bells, they richly ring

"And was that Lord our Christ the King ? "

St. Giles's bells they hear me call

I never knew the Lord at all.

Oh not in me your Saviour dwells

You ancient, rich St. Giles's bells.

Illuminated missals—spires—

Wide screens and decorated quires—

All these I loved, and on my knees

I thanked myself for knowing these
And watched the morning sunlight pass
Through richly stained Victorian glass
And in the colour-shafted air
I, kneeling, thought the Lord was there.
Now, lying in the gathering mist
I know that Lord did not exist
And lest this " I " should cease to be
Come, real Lord, come quick to me.
With every gust the chestnut sighs
With every breath a human dies
The man who smiled alone, alone
And went his journey on his own
With " Will you give my wife this letter,
In case, of course, I don't get better ? "
Waits for his coffin lid to close
On waxen head and yellow toes.
Almighty Saviour had I Faith
There'd be no fight with kindly Death.
Intolerably long and deep
St. Giles's bells swing on in sleep
" But still you go from here alone "
Say all the bells about the throne.

On Hearing the Full Peal of Ten Bells from Christ Church, Swindon, Wilts

Your peal of ten ring over then this town,
Ring on my men nor ever ring them down.
This winter chill, let sunset spill cold fire
On villa'd hill and on Sir Gilbert's spire,
So new, so high, so pure, so broach'd, so tall.
Long run the thunder of the bells through all !

Oh still white headstones on these fields of sound
Hear you the wedding joybells wheeling round ?
Oh brick-built breeding boxes of new souls,
Hear how the pealing through the louvres rolls !
Now birth and death-reminding bells ring clear,
Loud under 'planes and over changing gear.

Youth and Age on Beaulieu River, Hants

EARLY sun on Beaulieu water
　Lights the undersides of oaks,
Clumps of leaves it floods and blanches
All transparent glow the branches
　Which the double sunlight soaks ;
　And to her craft on Beaulieu water
　Clemency the General's daughter
　　Pulls across with even strokes.

Schoolboy sure she is this morning ;
　Soon her sharpie's rigg'd and free.
Cool beneath a garden awning
　Mrs. Fairclough sipping tea
And raising large long-distance glasses
As the little sharpie passes,
　Sighs our sailor girl to see :

Tulip figure, so appealing,
　Oval face, so serious-eyed,
Tree-roots pass'd and muddy beaches,
On to huge and lake-like reaches,

Soft and sun-warm, see her glide,
Slacks the slim young limbs revealing,
Sun-brown arm the tiller feeling,
Before the wind and with the tide.

Evening light will bring the water,
Day-long sun will burst the bud,
Clemency, the General's daughter,
Will return upon the flood.
But the older woman only
Knows the ebb tide leaves her lonely
With the shining fields of mud.

East Anglian Bathe

OH when the early morning at the seaside
  Took us with hurrying steps from Horsey
    Mere
To see the whistling bent-grass on the leeside
  And then the tumbled breaker line appear,
Oh, high the clouds with mighty adumbration
  Sailed over us to seaward fast and clear
And jellyfish in quivering isolation
  Lay silted in the dry sand of the breeze
And we, along the table-land of beach blown
  Went gooseflesh from our shoulders to our
    knees
And ran to catch the football, each to each
    thrown,
  In the soft and swirling music of the seas.

There splashed about our ankles as we waded
  Those intersecting wavelets morning cold,
And sudden dark a patch of sea was shaded,
  And sudden light, another patch would hold

EAST ANGLIAN BATHE

The warmth of whirling atoms in a sun-shot
  And underwater sandstorm green and gold.
So in we dived and louder than a gunshot
  Sea-water broke in fountains down the ear.
How cold the swim, how chattering cold the
    drying,
  How welcoming the inland reeds appear,
The woodsmoke and the breakfast and the
    frying,
  And your warm freshwater ripples, Horsey
  Mere.

Sunday Afternoon Service in St. Enodoc Church, Cornwall

COME on! come on! This hillock hides the
    spire
Now that one and now none. As winds
    about
The burnished path through lady's-finger,
    thyme
And bright varieties of saxifrage,
So grows the tinny tenor faint or loud
And all things draw towards St. Enodoc.
Come on! come on! and it is five to three.
Paths, unfamiliar to golfers' brogues,
Cross the eleventh fairway broadside on
And leave the fourteenth tee for thirteenth
    green,
Ignoring Royal and Ancient, bound for God.
Come on! come on! no longer bare of foot,
The sole grows hot in London shoes again
Jack Lambourne in his Sunday navy blue
Wears tie and collar, all from Selfridges.

There's Enid with a silly parasol,
And Graham in gray flannel with a crease
Across the middle of his coat which lay
Pressed 'neath the box of his Meccano set,
Sunday to Sunday.

       Goes, Come on ! come on !,
The tinny tenor. Hover flies remain
More than a moment on a ragwort bunch,
And peoples' passing shadows don't disturb
Red Admirals basking with their wings apart.

  A mile of sunny, empty sand away,
A mile of shallow pools and lugworm casts,
Safe, faint and surfy, beats the lowest tide.

  Even the villas have a Sunday look.
The Ransome mower's locked into the shed
" I have a splitting headache from the sun."
And bedroom windows flutter cheerful chintz
Where double-aspirined, a mother sleeps.
A father in a loggia reads a book,
Large, desultory, birthday-present size,
Published with coloured plates by *Country Life*
A Bernard Darwin on *The English Links*
Or Braid and Taylor on *The Mashie Shot.*

And so my thoughts this happy Sabbathtide.
Where deep cliffs loom enormous, where cascade
Mesembryanthemum and stone-crop down,
Where seagulls look no larger than a lark
Hung midway twixt the cliff-top and the sand,
Sun-shadowed valleys roll along the sea.
Forced by the backwash, see the nearest wave
Rise to a wall of huge, translucent green
And crumble into spray along the top
Blown seaward by the landbreeze. Now she breaks
And in an arch of thunder plunges down
To burst and tumble, foam on top of foam,
Criss-crossing, baffled, sucked and shot again
A waterfall of whiteness, down a rock,
Without a source but roller's furthest reach :
And tufts of sea-pink, high and dry for years,
Are flooded out of ledges, boulders seem
No bigger than a pebble washed about
In this tremendous tide. Oh kindly slate !
To give me shelter in this crevice dry.
These shivering stalks of bent-grass, lucky plant,

SUNDAY AFTERNOON SERVICE

Have better chance than I to last the storm.

Oh kindly slate of these unaltered cliffs,

Firm, barren substrate of our windy fields !

Oh lichened slate in walls, they knew your
   worth

Who raised you up to make this House of God

What faith was his, that dim, that Cornish
    saint,

Small rushlight of a long-forgotten church,

Who lived with God on this unfriendly shore,

Who knew He made the Atlantic and the
    stones

And destined seamen here to end their lives

Dashed on a rock, rolled over in the surf,

And not one hair forgotten. Now they lie

In centuries of sand beside the church.

Less pitiable are they than the corpse

Of a large golfer, only four weeks dead,

This sunlit and sea-distant afternoon.

" Praise ye the Lord ! " and in another key

The Lord's name by harmonium be praised.

" The Second Evening and the Fourteenth
    Psalm."

The Irish Unionist's Farewell to Greta Hellström in 1922

GOLDEN haired and golden hearted
  I would ever have you be,
As you were when last we parted
  Smiling slow and sad at me.
Oh! the fighting down of passion!
  Oh! the century-seeming pain—
Parting in this off-hand fashion
  In Dungarvan in the rain.

Slanting eyes of blue, unweeping,
  Stands my Swedish beauty where
Gusts of Irish rain are sweeping
  Round the statue in the square;
Corner boys against the walling
  Watch us furtively in vain,
And the Angelus is calling
  Through Dungarvan in the rain.

THE IRISH UNIONIST'S FAREWELL

Gales along the Commeragh Mountains,
　　Beating sleet on creaking signs,
Iron gutters turned to fountains,
　　And the windscreen laced with lines,
And the evening getting later,
　　And the ache—increased again,
As the distance grows the greater
　　From Dungarvan in the rain.

There is no one now to wonder
　　What eccentric sits in state
While the beech trees rock and thunder
　　Round his gate-lodge and his gate.
Gone—the ornamental plaster,
　　Gone—the overgrown demesne
And the car goes fast, and faster,
　　From Dungarvan in the rain.

Had I kissed and drawn you to me,
　　Had you yielded warm for cold,
What a power had pounded through me
　　As I stroked your streaming gold !

THE IRISH UNIONIST'S FAREWELL

You were right to keep us parted :
  Bound and parted we remain,
Aching, if unbroken hearted—
  Oh ! Dungarvan in the rain !

In Memory of Basil, Marquess of Dufferin and Ava

ON such a morning as this
  with the birds ricocheting their music
Out of the whelming elms
  to a copper beech's embrace
And a sifting sound of leaves
  from multitudinous branches
Running across the park
  to a chequer of light on the lake,
On such a morning as this
  with *The Times* for June the eleventh
Left with coffee and toast
  you opened the breakfast-room window
And, sprawled on the southward terrace, said :
  " That means war in September."

Friend of my youth, you are dead !
  and the long peal pours from the steeple
Over this sunlit quad
  in our University city
And soaks in Headington stone.
  Motionless stand the pinnacles.

IN MEMORY OF BASIL

Under a flying sky .
 as though they too listened and waited
Like me for your dear return
 with a Bullingdon noise of an evening
In a Sports-Bugatti from Thame
 that belonged to a man in Magdalen.
Friend of my youth, you are dead !
 and the quads are empty without you.

Then there were people about.
 Each hour, like an Oxford archway,
Opened on long green lawns
 and distant unvisited buildings
And you my friend were explorer
 and so you remained to me always
Humorous, reckless, loyal—
 my kind, heavy-lidded companion.
Stop, oh many bells, stop
 pouring on roses and creeper
Your unremembering peal
 this hollow, unhallowed V.E. day,—
I am deaf to your notes and dead
 by a soldier's body in Burma.